what would you ask?

MICHAEL FARADAY

Anita Ganeri
Illustrated by Neil Reed

Thameside Press

Distributed in the United States by
Smart Apple Media
1980 Lookout Drive
North Mankato, MN 56003

Text copyright © Anita Ganeri 2000

Printed in the USA

Editor: Veronica Ross
Designer: Caroline Grimshaw
Illustrator: Neil Reed
Consultants: Hester Collicutt and Alison Porter

Library of Congress Cataloging-in-Publication Data

Ganeri, Anita, 1961-
    Michael Faraday / by Anita Ganeri.
        p. cm. -- (What would you ask?)
    Includes index.
    Summary: A biography of the nineteenth-century British scientist who worked
with electricity, told in the form of an imagined interview.
    ISBN 1-929298-77-3
    1. Faraday, Michael, 1791-1867--Juvenile literature. 2. Physicists--Great Britain--
Biography--Juvenile literature. [1. Faraday, Michael, 1791-1867. 2. Physicists.]
I. Title.

QC16.F2 G36 2000
530'.092--dc21
[B]   00-022318

9 8 7 6 5 4 3 2 1

Contents

What do you do?   4

Where were you born?   6

Did you go to school?   8

How did you become a scientist?   10

Who trained you to be a scientist?   12

What sort of work did you do?   14

What was your greatest discovery?   16

How many experiments did you do?   18

Did you get married?   20

How did you help make science more popular?   22

When did you retire?   24

How is Michael Faraday remembered today?   26

Some important dates   28

Glossary   30

Index   32

What do you do?

"I am a scientist. I discovered many important things about electricity."

Think of all the ways in which you use electricity. How would you manage without it? We use electricity for light and heat, and to cook our food. It also powers the electrical gadgets we rely on in our everyday lives.

Every time you switch on the television or turn on your computer, you should feel grateful to the pioneering Michael Faraday. His work made it possible for electricity to be brought to our homes, schools, shops, and factories. Michael Faraday is sometimes called "the father of electricity." Without him, our lives might be very different.

Michael did not set out to become a scientist. When he was young, he worked as a bookbinder to earn money for his family. There was no time left over for going to school or college. Yet, despite his humble beginnings, Michael Faraday went on to become one of the greatest scientists of all.

Where were you born?

"I was born in Surrey, England."

Michael Faraday was born on September 22, 1791 in Newington Butts, Surrey, England. This is now part of London. His father, James, was a blacksmith who had moved to Surrey from the north of England in the hope of finding work. He died in 1810, when Michael was 19 years old.

Michael was one of four children.
He had an elder sister, Elizabeth,
and an elder brother, Robert.
Next came Michael, then his
younger sister, Margaret.
The family had little money
and the children were always
hungry. Sometimes, a loaf of
bread had to last for a week.
When Michael's father died,
his mother (Margaret) took
in lodgers to help pay
their way. From an early
age, Robert and Michael
went out to work and
gave their wages
to their mother.

7

Did you go to school?

"Yes, but not for very long.
I left school when I was 13."

Michael left school when he was 13 years old.
All he had learned was basic reading, writing,
and mathematics. Even when he became
a famous scientist, he was still not very
good at mathematics.

Michael went to work as an errand boy in
a bookstore. He delivered newspapers and
books, and did odd jobs. After a year the
bookstore owner, Mr. Riebau, took him
on as his apprentice. For the next seven
years, he trained Michael to become
a bookbinder. In those days, people
took books and magazines to
stores like Mr. Riebau's for
binding in leather.

Michael loved reading the books that came into the shop. He learned about chemistry from a book called *The Elements of Chemistry* by Mrs. Marcet and about electricity from the *Encyclopedia Britannica*. In his spare time, Michael started doing simple experiments. He made an electrical machine from bits and pieces he found at home, including old bottles and scraps of wood.

How did you become a scientist?

"By luck, I was given some tickets to a science lecture."

One of Mr. Riebau's customers was impressed by Michael's interest in science. He gave Michael tickets for a series of lectures at the Royal Institution in London. The talks were to be given by Sir Humphry Davy, one of the most famous scientists of the time and Professor of Chemistry at the Royal Institution.

The Royal Institution was set up by an American scientist in 1799. Apart from its lecture theater, it had a well-stocked library and science laboratories. Soon it was a leading center for science and research. It is still going strong today.

Michael was thrilled. He sat through the lectures making notes. Afterward, he took the notes back to Mr. Riebau's shop and bound them into a book. He sent the book to Sir Humphry Davy with a letter asking to be remembered if Sir Humphry ever needed an assistant.

Who trained you to be a scientist?

"A famous scientist called Sir Humphry Davy."

A year later, in March, 1813, Michael's dream of becoming a scientist took a giant step forward. A laboratory assistant at the Royal Institution was sacked for fighting. Sir Humphry Davy sent for Michael and offered him the job. The salary equaled about $4 a week and Michael was given two rooms to live in at the Royal Institution. He was only too happy to accept.

Michael began by helping Sir Humphry with his experiments. Then, in October, Sir Humphry decided to go on a tour of Europe and offered to take Michael with him. It was the chance of a lifetime. Michael had never left London before, let alone traveled abroad.

The tour lasted for 18 months. The party visited France, Switzerland, and Italy. Michael wrote everything down in his diary. He did not like Sir Humphry's wife, who treated him like a servant—but the people he met made up for his poor treatment. Among them were two of the most famous scientists of the day, Alessandro Volta and André Marie Ampère. Both were famous for their work in electricity.

What sort of work did you do?

"At first I did many experiments in chemistry."

Back in London, Michael continued to work as Sir Humphry's assistant. He helped Sir Humphry with his famous invention of a safety lamp for miners. Michael also taught himself more about chemistry. He spent hours reading books and studying scientific journals in the Royal Institution's library.

Before long, Michael began work on his own chemistry experiments. He made some amazing discoveries. In 1823, he was the first person to turn chlorine gas into a liquid. A year later, he discovered a new chemical called benzene, which is still very important in industry for making medicines, perfumes, and dyes. He also made an early type of stainless steel.

Michael soon became a respected scientist. In 1824, he was promoted to Superintendent of the House and Laboratory at the Royal Institution. Many organizations asked him for scientific advice. However, Michael's thoughts were turning elsewhere, to the subject of electricity.

What was your greatest discovery?

"I found an amazing link between electricity and magnetism."

In 1820, a Danish scientist called Hans Christian Oersted found that he could use electricity to produce magnetism. Michael also began to think about electricity and magnetism. In 1821, he discovered a way of making electricity and magnetism work together to produce movement—inventing the first electric motor.

In 1831, Michael invented the transformer. This is a device that changes the voltage (energy) of electricity from high to low, or vice versa. He also argued that if electricity could produce magnetism, then the opposite might also be true. It should be possible to use magnetism to produce electricity. A few months later, he used this idea to invent the first dynamo.

Michael called the link between electricity and magnetism electromagnetic induction. His discovery of the principles behind the electric motor, the transformer, and the dynamo made it possible for us to have an electricity supply in our homes today.

How many experiments did you do?

"An awful lot! I did thousands of experiments."

Throughout his career, Michael carried out thousands of experiments in his laboratory in the basement of the Royal Institution. He believed that scientists should always test out their theories thoroughly before they made them known. That way, they could be sure of the facts. He constantly checked and re-checked his ideas before he told anyone about them.

Michael kept detailed notes of all his experiments from the time he arrived at the Royal Institution right up to his last experiment in 1862. He also drew sketches of what he had done. Perhaps his greatest experiment was done on August 29, 1831 when he discovered electromagnetic induction. Michael knew that this was the start of something special. To mark this, he began a new numbering system for his experiments—starting again at number one.

Did you get married?

"Yes. My wife was called Sarah."

In 1820, Michael became engaged to Sarah Barnard, the daughter of a silversmith. They were married a year later and lived in a flat in the Royal Institution. It was a long and happy marriage.

Michael and Sarah lived a simple life. They had many friends but rarely went out to parties or dinners. Michael preferred to get on with his work.

Michael and Sarah were Christians, belonging to the Sandemanian Church. Their religion was very important to them. But some of the rules of the Church were very strict. In 1840, Michael became an elder, or senior member, of the Church. But a few years later, he missed a Sunday service because he had been invited to dine with Queen Victoria. He was dismissed from the Church and only allowed to rejoin many years later.

How did you help make science more popular?

"I gave lectures to adults and children."

Michael started a series of weekly lectures at the Royal Institution to help people understand science. The lectures were held on a Friday night. They began at 9p.m. and lasted for one hour. The speaker was always an important scientist. Michael gave many of the Friday lectures himself.

Michael also started a series of Christmas lectures for children. He was a brilliant speaker, so impressing Queen Victoria's husband, Prince Albert, that the prince brought his children to hear him speak.

Michael's most famous Christmas lecture was called *The Chemical History of a Candle*. Using an ordinary candle, he explained its chemistry in simple terms. What was it made of and how did it burn? Why was its flame a particular shape? The lecture was so popular it was repeated several times.

The Friday night lectures and the Christmas lectures are still held today. In Great Britain, the Christmas lectures are shown on TV.

23

When did you retire?

"I left the Royal Institution in 1865."

From about 1855, Michael's health began to break down. He suffered from spells of dizziness and kept losing his memory. In 1861, Michael gave up the Christmas lectures. Later, he resigned from the rest of his duties. It was a very hard decision to make. He had spent more than 50 years living at the Royal Institution. It had been his home and his life's work.

To reward Michael for his scientific achievements, Queen Victoria gave him the use of a fine house in Hampton Court, south of London. In 1862, he and Sarah moved from their flat in the Royal Institution to live there.

On August 25, 1867, Michael Faraday died peacefully in his armchair. He was 76 years old. He is buried in a simple grave in Highgate Cemetery in London. The plain headstone gives only his name and the dates of his birth and death.

How is Michael Faraday remembered today?

From humble beginnings, Michael Faraday became one of the greatest scientists of his day. He is best remembered for his work in electricity, particularly for his electric motor, transformer, and dynamo.

Electric motors are used in hundreds of electrical gadgets, from hairdryers to vacuum cleaners. When you plug your CD player into a socket, electricity passes through the electric motor producing movement. This makes the CD spin round.

Plugging your CD player in connects it to the mains electricity supply. This comes to your home from a power plant.

Dynamos and transformers make this possible. Dynamos work in the opposite way to electric motors. A dynamo converts movement into an electrical current. Inside a dynamo, a wire is moved in a magnetic field and this makes an electric current flow through the wire. The electric generator that we know today is based on this principle. It generates (makes) electricity which can then be sent to your home. Transformers change the voltage (energy) of electricity. They make sure that the electricity reaching your home is safe to use.

We often take electricity for granted. But next time you turn on the light or switch on the television, remember that it was Michael Faraday who made this possible.

Some important dates

1791 Michael Faraday is born in Surrey, near London.

1799 The Royal Institution is founded in London.

1804 Faraday leaves school and goes to work in Mr. Riebau's bookstore as a paper boy.

1805 Mr. Riebau takes Faraday on as an apprentice bookbinder. His apprenticeship lasts for seven years.

1812 Faraday hears Sir Humphry Davy lecture at the Royal Institution. His apprenticeship comes to an end.

1813 In March, Faraday becomes Davy's laboratory assistant at the Royal Institution. In October, he accompanies Davy on a grand tour of Europe.

1815 Faraday and Davy return to England. Faraday continues work at the Royal Institution.

1816 Faraday gives his first lecture at the Royal Institution and publishes his first scientific paper.

1820 Faraday stops working for Davy and starts his own research. He quickly gains a reputation as a brilliant chemist.

1821 Faraday marries Sarah Barnard. The couple live in a flat in the Royal Institution. He begins to experiment with electricity.

1824 Faraday discovers the chemical benzene. He is appointed Director of the Laboratory. He starts giving the Friday evening lectures at the Royal Institution. They continue today.

1827 The Christmas lectures for children begin at the Royal Institution. They also continue today.

1831 In August, Faraday performs his most famous experiment and discovers the principle of electromagnetic induction.

1832 Faraday proves that electricity is always the same whatever its source.

1833 Faraday becomes Fallerian Professor of Chemistry at the Royal Institution. He devises new scientific words to describe his new discoveries.

1840 Faraday becomes an elder of the Sandemanian Church.

1841 Faraday's health breaks down and he takes an eight-month vacation in Switzerland.

1844 Faraday is dismissed as an elder of his church for dining with Queen Victoria on a Sunday. He is reinstated in 1869.

1858 Queen Victoria gives Faraday a house at Hampton Court. She offers him a knighthood but he refuses it. He says that he prefers to remain plain Mr. Faraday.

1861 Faraday resigns from giving the Christmas lectures.

1865 Faraday resigns from all his duties at the Royal Institution.

1867 Faraday dies on August 25. He is buried in Highgate Cemetery, in London.

1881 The first public electricity supply is set up at Godalming, in Surrey (near London).

Glossary

André Marie Ampère A famous French scientist who lived from 1775–1836. His work looked at the connection between electricity and magnetism.

apprentice Someone who learns a craft or trade from a skilled person while working for them.

chemistry The study of chemicals and how they behave. Chemicals are substances found in solid, liquid, or gas form. They change when mixed with other chemicals.

chlorine gas The gas form of the chemical, chlorine.

Sir Humphry Davy A famous British chemist and physicist who lived from 1778–1829. He invented the safety lamp for miners.

dynamo A machine which turns movement into electricity. Inside a dynamo, a wire is moved in a magnetic field and this makes an electric current flow in the wire.

electric current The flow of electricity through a wire or wires.

electric motor A machine which uses electricity and magnetism to produce movement. Electric motors are used in many everyday items, such as CD players.

electromagnetic induction The link between electricity and magnetism. Faraday produced magnetism from electricity, and electricity from magnetism.

generator A machine that makes electricity from another form of energy, such as the heat given off by burning coal or oil.

humble Very modest or simple.

magnetic field The area around a magnet in which objects are affected by a magnetic force.

magnetism A force produced by a magnet, or by an electric current. It can attract, repel (push away), or change substances from a distance.

mains electricity The electricity made in a power plant and supplied to our homes, schools, hospitals, offices, and factories.

pioneer Someone who starts something or comes up with a new idea or invention.

power plant A factory-like building where electricity is produced from coal, gas, oil, or nuclear power and supplied to customers.

safety lamp A lamp invented by Sir Humphry Davy which saved the lives of many miners. Its design stopped the flame from setting fire to explosive gas found in mines.

transformer The voltage (energy) of electricity from generators in a power plant is increased by transformers before it transfers to power cables that carry it around the country. The voltage is decreased by another transformer as it is transferred from the power cables to households.

Alessandro Volta An Italian scientist who lived from 1745–1827. He made many important discoveries about electricity.

voltage The force that pushes an electric current along. It is measured in units called volts (V), which are named after Alessandro Volta.

Index

Ampère, André Marie 13, 30
apprenticeship 8, 28, 30

Barnard, Sarah 20, 28
benzene experiments 14, 28
bookbinding work 8–9, 28

Chemical History of a Candle, The 23
chemistry 9, 14, 28, 30
chlorine gas experiments 14, 30
Christian beliefs 20
Christmas Lectures 22–23, 29
Church rules 20, 29

Davy, Sir Humphry 10, 12–14,
  28, 30
dynamos 16, 26–27, 30

electric current 27, 30
electric motors 16, 26, 30
electricity 4, 9, 16, 26, 28–29
electromagnetic induction 16, 19,
  29–30
European tour 13, 28
experiments 9, 14, 16, 18-19, 26–29

"father of electricity" 4
Friday evening lectures 22, 28

generators 27, 30
Hampton Court 24, 29

laboratory assistant job 12, 14, 28
lectures at the Royal Institution 10,
  22–23, 28–29

magnetism 16, 31
Michael's childhood 6–9, 28
Michael's death 24, 29
Michael's education 8
Michael's family 6–7
Michael's health 24, 29
Michael's marriage 20, 28
Michael's retirement 24, 29

Oersted, Hans Christian 16

public electricity supply 29

Religious beliefs 20
Riebau, Mr. 8, 10, 28
Royal Institution 10, 12, 22–23,
  24, 28–29

safety lamp invention 14, 31
Sandemanian Church 20, 29
science lectures 10, 22–23, 28–29
stainless steel 14
Superintendent job 15

transformers 16, 26–27, 31

Victoria, Queen 24, 29
Volta, Alessandro 13, 31
voltage experiments 16, 31